Growing Strawberries

by Sarah Tatler

Table of Contents

What Is a Strawberry?

A strawberry is a fruit. Some strawberries are big and some are little.

⬆ Most strawberries are bright red.

🎧 There are over 200 seeds on a strawberry.

Take a closer look at a strawberry.

It has seeds on the outside.
Can you see the tiny seeds?

Strawberries grow on strawberry plants on the ground. They get their beautiful red color as they grow ripe.

⬆ People pick strawberries when they are ripe.

↑ People can buy strawberries at a
market like this.

Here are some boxes of bright
red strawberries. They are sweet
and juicy! Lots of people buy
strawberries to eat.

How Do Strawberries Grow?

Strawberry plants need lots of sun. Long stems called runners grow close to the ground. A new strawberry plant grows from each runner.

Look at the parts of a strawberry plant. Find the beautiful flower. Then find the fruit.

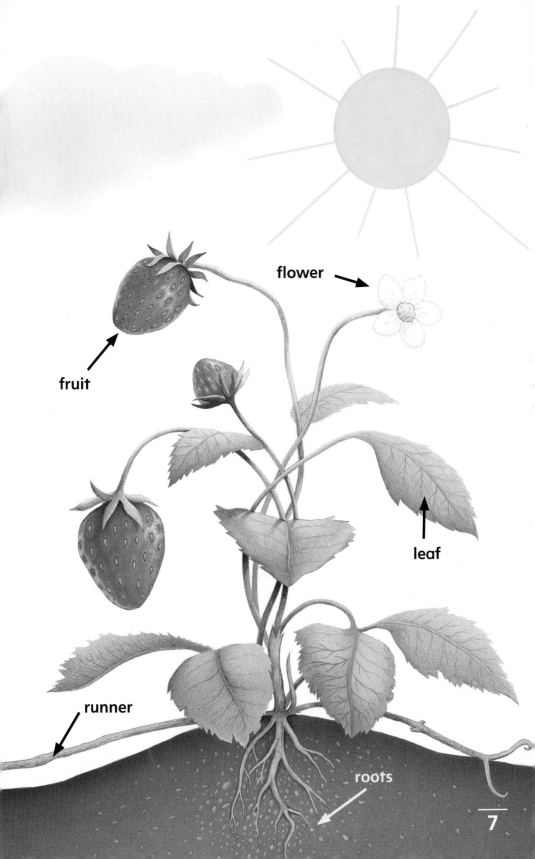

fruit

flower

leaf

runner

roots

Strawberries are easy plants to grow.

1. First find a place that gets at least six hours of sun.

2. Next dig holes for the little plants. Put the holes 12 inches apart. They should not be crowded together.

3. Put the plants in the holes. Press the soil around each plant. Make sure the soil covers the tops of the roots.

4. Next water the plants.

5. Pick the strawberries when they are ripe.

Animals like strawberries. As your plants grow, you will need to watch for animals. Birds, turtles, and bugs eat strawberry plants. It's easy for an animal to eat the fruit and nibble on the leaves.

↑ This turtle looks for strawberries to eat.

Nets can help keep birds away from strawberry plants. A small fence can help keep little animals away.

Who Likes Strawberries?

Many people like strawberries.
People can grow strawberries
in most parts of the United States.

The United States of America

⬆ The states where farmers
grow the most strawberries
are colored in red.

This is a strawberry farm.

⬆ This boy likes to have strawberries on his cereal.

Strawberries are fun to eat. Some people dip strawberries in cream. Some people use them to make strawberry jam.

Of course, the best way to eat a strawberry is to pop one in your mouth.

Comprehension Check

Retell

Use a Classify and Categorize Chart to sort fruits by color.

Red Fruits	Yellow Fruits
1	1
2	2
3	3

Think and Compare

1. Look back at page 11. How can you keep birds and other little animals away from your strawberry plants?

2. Have you ever eaten strawberries? Do you like them? Why or why not?

3. Does growing strawberries look easy? Explain your answer.